POSTCARDS FROM POLAND
and other correspondences

POSTCARDS FROM POLAND
and other correspondences

Maria Jastrzębska
and Jola Scicińska

WORKING PRESS
Books by and about working class artists

POSTCARDS FROM POLAND and other correspondences
Maria Jastrzębska and Jola Scicińska

WORKING PRESS books by and about working class artists

Published by Working Press, 85 St Agnes Place, Kennington, London SEI 4BB.

Typeset by Community Copyart, 41 Culross Buildings, Battlebridge Road, Kings Cross, London NWI 2TH.

Printed and bound by Hollen St Press Ltd, 141/3 Farnham Road, Slough, Berks., SLI 4XB.

PRODUCED WITH THE SUPPORT OF NORTH LONDON LESBIAN
STRENGTH AND GAY PRIDE AND THE HACKNEY WOMEN'S UNIT.

ISBN 1 870736 06 0

OUR WARMEST THANKS TO EVERYONE WHO HELPED MAKE THIS BOOK POSSIBLE

to our families for their wealth of experience and historical knowledge

to Community Copyart without whose unique resources this book would have been a lot less interesting

to the workers there for being helpful and friendly and in particular Carl Halksworth whose knowledge, skillful touch on the computer and interest in our project have been indispensable

to Helen Salkin for her energy, enthusiasm, typing and keen literary eye

to Helen Morgan for her openness and generosity and friendship

to Bob Jackman for providing innumerable hot dinners, doing essential driving, having a bendable ear and for more support than he ever got credit for

to Ela Ginalska for giving freely of her time and expertise

to Helen Palmer for useful feedback especially in the initial stages

to Polskie Feministki for existing despite the odds

to everyone who has given Maria much needed practical, spiritual and emotional help throughout her illness

to four black cats whose idea of help is to tread on things and tear them up, but who have been good company nonetheless

and to Josh the dog who would have left his paw prints everywhere, if only he'd been allowed to.

before

Queuing and queuing

nothing to write home about
nothing exotic
about poverty
just peeling paint
brick broken up
rust, rotting fabric
streaks and smudges of grey
ground into lines of tiredness
on the forgotten faces
of Europe's poorest relations
everything to write home about

WSZYSCY JESTEŚMY ODPOWIEDZIALNI ZA POLSKĘ

4

Not begging but trying to sell

in the subway
people with outstretched arms
stand along a blurred line
between what's legal
and what the police can be bribed
to overlook
not begging but trying to sell
anything
from plastic windmills for the kids
Western-looking denim jackets
electric mixers
to herringbone brassières
single garments
or worn old shoes

dirty pink beige
endless grey
the colours of concrete
spread to the edges
of the city

we are all responsible for Poland

WSZYSCY JESTEŚMY ODPOWIEDZIALNI ZA POLSKĘ

6

Hard currency forest

look at the feet
you can always tell
by the shoes
badly made, worn right down

I look at the eyes
I imagine forests
cut down
sold for export
to countries which preserve
their own vegetation

one night
stopped at a railway station
seeing bales of timber
soaked by rain
the brown trains
stand waiting on silver black lines
you are further from me
than all geography
across borders
not even charted anywhere
such distances to cover
before we meet

WSZYSCY JESTEŚMY ODPOWIEDZIALNI ZA POLSKĘ

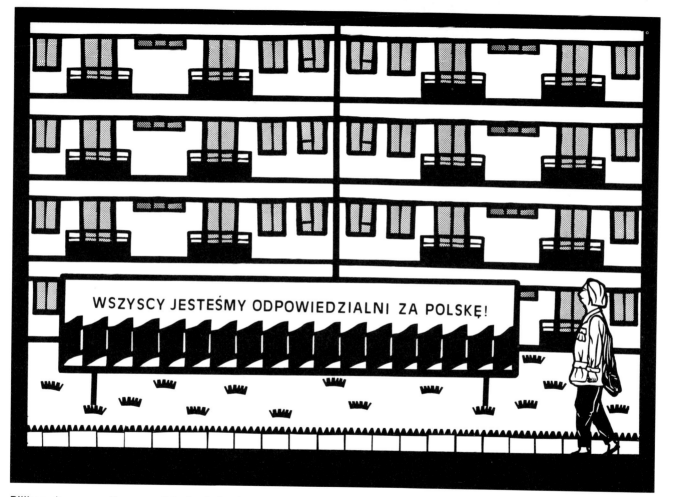

Billboard: we are all responsible for Poland

no one tries to sell me
tobacco, fast cars, booze, or Coca-Cola
on bill boards
it's a relief not to see
women's bodies displayed
on every corner
but even in the quietest country lanes
in huge letters
of faded white and red
it says instead
serve the motherland and the party
build socialism
with hard work and principles
we are all responsible
for Poland

WSZYSCY JESTEŚMY ODPOWIEDZIALNI ZA POLSKĘ

Fighting imaginary Germans

I grew up
turning the pages of a big book
filled with photographs
of children wearing helmets
no uniforms, just armbands,
carrying guns, smiling

I played in an English garden
filled with rhododendrons
and fruit trees
fighting imaginary Germans

some days
crossing these streets
I dodge among flames
no one else notices

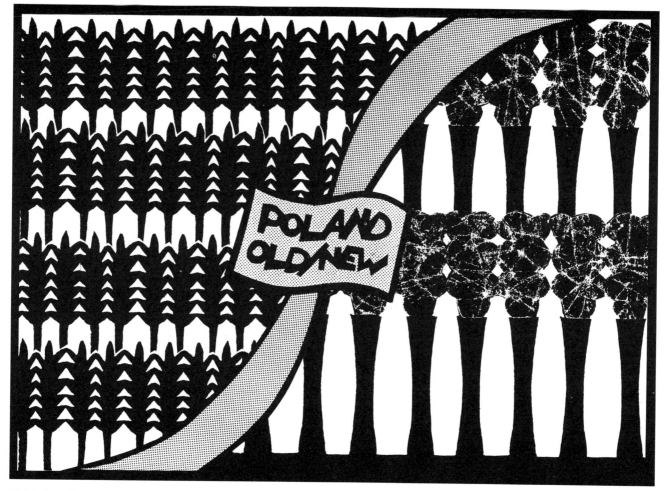

Fields into factories

my aunts cook me pancakes
track down books of poetry for me
long sold out
my uncle gives me a map
sold out, too, years ago
never reprinted
my friends look at one another
when I say my stomach is upset
she's not used to the water
like us
they give me spring water to drink
instead of water from the tap

eating curd cheese
on rye bread
that you can really chew
with tomatoes and fresh dill
on a plain linen table cloth

in a room
where the bookshelves
crammed high
reach right to the ceiling
and there are wool hangings on the wall
I wonder why I did not come here sooner
but it is not always easy
to make the journey back
we know so little
about each other's lives
hurry to fill the gaps
sometimes with endless talking
politics and history
sometimes with gifts or laughter
some gaps
we don't know how to fill
they remain

WSZYSCY JESTEŚMY ODPOWIEDZIALNI ZA POLSKĘ

A Gift From Our Neighbours

friends laugh
when I look
for news of opposition
in the papers
accustomed to wading through
pages of mud-slinging and titillation
or at least a distortion of the facts
not expecting to meet
an avalanche of silence

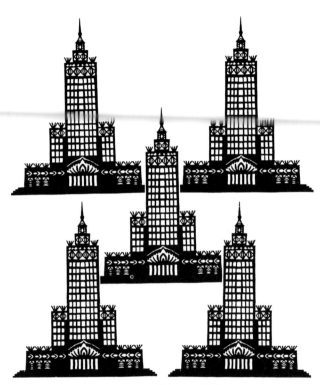

Moscow Has Many

'what makes me sick
is some Westerner
preaching to me
about the virtues of socialism
treating me like his white negro
too backward to work it out
for myself
can't they see we're the subject
of this experiment
while they sit pretty
over there in their Western homes'

16

Wrocław: school of medicine

ORANGE PEEL

my cousin notices immediately
'she's left it all, look!'
sugared orange peel
on the side of my plate
proof of everything
I've learnt to take for granted

the bittersweet taste
I pushed away as a child
English marmalade on toast
breakfasts in an unknown country
making mistakes
as I do now
as an adult this time
back again after years
here, where oranges
cost so much

Do you now have to be a Catholic to be Polish?

we travelled together
on the same plane
but on different passports
hers Polish, mine British
sometimes I wonder if we've landed
in different countries

on the plane
she seemed happier
than she'd been in months
yet the excitement of homecoming
soon wore off

she is more at home here
than I'll ever be
but because of this
much more on trial
each night the faces
of family and friends she grew up with
come to sit in judgement over her
why did you leave us
what have you made of your life
they always ask

Arrival

ARRIVAL

as the plane touched down
I noticed the soldiers
hanging about outside the airport

once inside
everyone was swearing and arguing
ganging up against the most brazen
of the queue-jumpers
we got separated straight away

porters pushed their trolleys
with astonishing grace
and saintly self-restraint
through a shifting wall of people
'stand back!' yelled the customs men

we hurled ourselves
into this fray
looking for chinks –
someone to let us through

behind the glass
her mother
a small resolute figure
stood her ground
among the jostling bodies
waved and held up the dog in her arms
for us to see

in the middle of the one clear gangway
people stopped to embrace
dropped all their luggage, stood quite still
in tears of relief
everyone seemed to be carrying flowers

we were through
we kept losing and finding each other
in the crowds
she handed me an orchid
from her mother

then I was being whisked away
by a cousin I'd never met before
striding with ease through the throng
like a forester crossing familiar thickets
he carried my rucksack

in the car I was being asked
hundreds of questions
what was it I wanted to do
in this country of theirs
I never did explain who she was

TRAVELLING BACK IN TIME

I have found myself
travelling back in time
leaving behind
barely begun spring
the promise of yellow daffodils
back to bare trees
to buds under siege
from the frost

rummaging
through someone else's kitchen
looking for plates or pans
in unfamiliar places
strange cupboards
someone else's crucifix
hangs on the wall
above my head

somebody's unmarried daughter
stripped bare
like the trees
of everything I'm used to being
or know for certain
standing in someone else's shoes
they are not comfortable

but a map of the world
on the large black and white TV
without England at its centre
brings me such simple relief
and joy
reminds me
why I've come

Plac Zamkowy, Warsaw: rebuilt from ruins, with plaque commemorating civilians shot by nazis

WALKING THROUGH STREETS

I am back
in a place I'd almost written off
like a bad debt
but at the same time
a long-standing obligation
I'm crossing bridges
burnt long ago

was it here my grandparents
searched for my uncle's
missing body
after the Warsaw Uprising
my father's kid brother
whose face I know
only from photographs

WSZYSCY JESTEŚMY ODPOWIEDZIALNI ZA POLSKĘ

walking through streets
my parents knew like their pockets
inside out
holding a map in my hand
recognising names I once heard in passing
or in stories
I get lost many times
ask directions again and again
this always happens to me
in unknown places

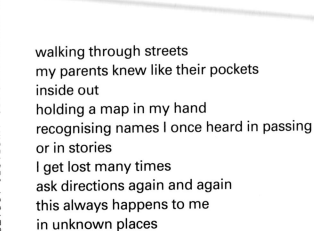

Best friends

it is colder here
at this time of year
hyacinths aren't out
we are different here
women link arms
friends embrace
mothers and children hold hands
girls plait and stroke
each other's hair
men kiss one another on the cheek
they kiss women's hands
but we walk apart

grown women
pressed back
into childhood
stooping as we enter
a lilliput land
rooms tiny as cells
where dreams and nightmares
call across the years to us

suddenly I'm half my age again
even on the phone
we whisper to one another
talk in code
like adolescents
I can't believe I've come back
so far

this is how I grew up
learning to play a closed hand
hiding trumps in my sleeve
love's smell on my fingers
heartaches behind smiles
smiles behind hands

even out in the open
in meadows, woodlands
always looking over one shoulder
careful
in any new place
double-checking the lock on the door

WSZYSCY JESTEŚMY ODPOWIEDZIALNI ZA POLSKĘ

28

Still best friends?

be quiet, she hisses
when I raise my voice
in the street
she's sure someone's looking at us
they're not, of course
but she's right
for a moment I'd forgotten
where I was
in this country
where everything's the other way around
where everyone speaks like us
and Polish isn't our secret code any more
where everyone I meet
shakes my hand
without thinking it strange
where any child can pronounce my name
where I feel so welcome
and so alone

WSZYSCY JESTEŚMY ODPOWIEDZIALNI ZA POLSKĘ

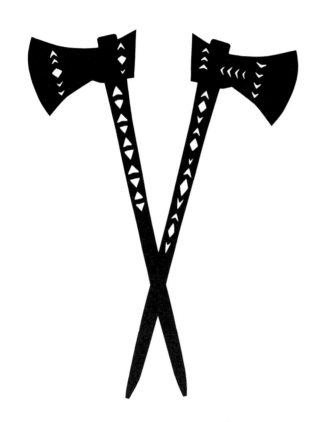

I kiss all her friends
who don't know
they ask: how are you enjoying yourself
in Poland?
I'd like to say
sometimes it feels
as though I'm walking on the moon
here I am already fluent in Polish
but it isn't enough
and often I think of my parents
arriving in England
having to start from scratch

I'd like to say
look I'm not her flat-mate
I'm the one she loves
leaves sweet silly notes
on the pillow for
only lately whenever I reach out
to touch her
she shrinks back

do you think when she cracks
all those jokes
that she's happy
or is she running on the spot
afraid to stop

I don't say any of those things
I become rather tongue-tied
besides, my Polish feels too formal
not colloquial enough
perhaps her friends find me serious
or quiet

with those in the know
I feel like a gay ambassador
burdened with the responsibility
of representing not only myself
but a way of life
I'm a queer fish
in a goldfish bowl
am I presentable enough
and who the hell
can we tell
when things go wrong?

before I left
my mother said
don't go on any demonstrations
you don't know what it's like
the militia over there

but in fact the only demonstration I've been on
the police kept out of sight
low profile to impress
prominent Jewish visitors from the West
invited to the official commemoration
of the Ghetto Uprising

this demonstration wasn't advertised
anywhere, but somehow people knew about it
it's the unofficial march to Umschlagplatz
from where the trains once took people away
never to bring them back
where it's taken so long
to get any monument put up

and it's my family
who bring me on this march
I think of all the times in London
facing the boys in blue
no family with me then
or perhaps a different kind of family

such a mix of old and young here
Jews and gentiles together too
lots of outlawed Solidarność banners
which you normally only see
inside certain churches
I peer through the crowd
to see who the speakers are
Marek Edelman is there
no government niceties for him
(unless you count the men in very boring suits
who watch his house so patiently)
the sole survivor of the Uprising HQ

an ordinary, home-grown Polish Jew
not a wealthy Westerner at all
right in their own backyard
how they must hate him
those in authority
for still commanding
human respect

it seems to me the Poles
do more talking than the Jews
a familiar pattern
I know from British demonstrations
where people speak on behalf of others
instead of giving them a voice
the flowers have been laid
a rabbi says Kaddish

hoping, in the usual way,
there won't be any incidents
we start to make our way home

Small town shop

PLASTIC BAGS

she's always telling me off
for leaving books open
with their spines bent back
for not straightening the seams
on my T-shirts – of all things –
when I wash my clothes
it drives me mad
how fussy she is

one day on the washing line
in the bathroom
of someone's apartment
I notice a row of plastic carrier bags
hanging up to dry

I think of my mother
hoarding each paper or plastic bag
every rubber band or piece of string

after years of living in England
she hasn't got used
to the throw-away mentality either

the streets are cleaner here
it's not because people are tidier
only there's less to discard

books are more fragile here
like rare flowers
they fall apart so easily
printed on cheaper paper
they're expensive
but people still buy them
and treasure them for years

WSZYSCY JESTEŚMY ODPOWIEDZIALNI ZA POLSKĘ

36

Small town with bicycle

a letter from England
tells me Section 28 has been passed
L writes: they're trying to silence us
the clocks are being turned back
on years of achievement
years out of our lives
how to reply?

Dear L
I have travelled even further back
to a silence so deep
it hurts
inside your bones

yet the longer I'm here
the closer I'm getting
to somewhere –
nothing makes sense any more
is it possible to travel backwards
and forwards
at one and the same time

Dear L
everyone here
seems to have dogs
if they're big
they have to wear muzzles
on public transport
you know, in Bulgaria
they aren't allowed to keep dogs
so they don't need muzzles
do they

there'd be no need
for a Section like 28 here
nobody's outspoken enough
at best we're seen as medical cases
either that
or the work of the devil
still, he's quite popular here
maybe we're in with a chance

38

The mermaid guards Warsaw, my dad's home town

Warsaw airport
waiting for M's flight from London
holding an aster in my hand
one of the crowd
feeling quite at home
now I've learnt my way around a bit
I can show off when she arrives
she's bringing supplies
luxuries like toilet paper –
the soft tissue kind –
magazines maybe some news or gossip
a second pair of eyes

Snowflakes and crocuses

A CARPET OF CROCUSES

snowflakes coat her eyelashes
under them her eyes shine
with delight
mirror my own

in the valley
where the snow has melted
a carpet of crocuses
springs up
tiny flames of purple and lilac

I've borrowed my cousin's gaiters
her woolly hat and mittens
my auntie is leading the way
through an enchanted silver forest
everything seems suddenly simpler
and more possible among friends
friends can touch

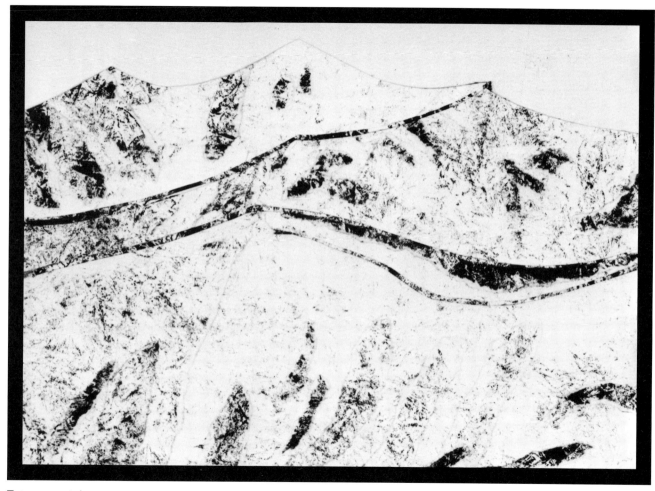

Tatry mountains

TATRY

our strides lengthen
among these snowclad giants
here in the mountains
I used to describe
in English compositions at school
without ever having seen them
never a doubt in my mind
they had to be the most beautiful
in the world

yet only a few metres away,
we're told, a young woman lies buried
killed skiing earlier this season
by an avalanche
they will have to wait
till all the snow melts
to uncover her body

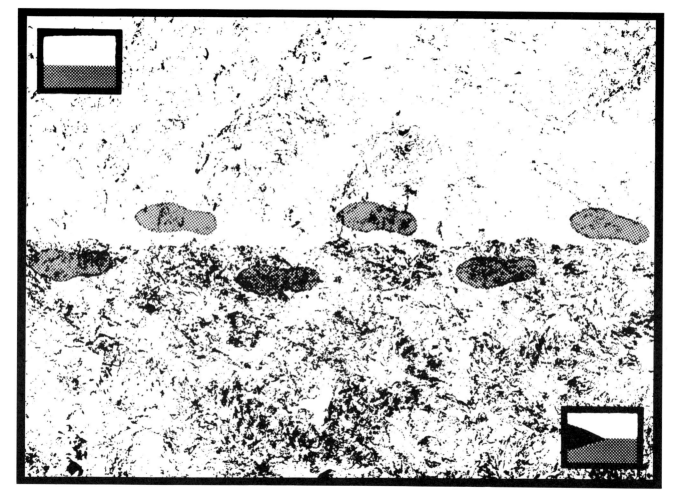

Footprints in the snow

ALONG THE BORDER

we're actually walking along the border
one foot inside Poland
the other outside
making tracks in the fresh snow
with our boots
I want to laugh
it seems hysterically funny
maybe it's the air
breathing great gulps of it
or maybe
it's because I've always lived like this
treading a fine line

Pope John Paul came to pray
in these mountains
Czechoslovak and Polish dissidents
picnicked beside this border
in summer sharing food and drink
exchanging ideas

we are four women on holiday
not a newsworthy event
four specks on the sleeve
of a giant's white shirt
spanning different generations
the East – West divide
exchanging views and sharing our supplies
we climb as far as we can
staying clear of paths
that are too dangerous

in the land of my childhood dreams
amazed at the boldness of crocuses
the perseverance of shrubs
springing straight out of sheer rock
knee deep in snow
I am warm for the first time

WSZYSCY JESTEŚMY ODPOWIEDZIALNI ZA POLSKĘ

46

Dorożka (drynda) - horse-drawn taxi

this is me
like any tourist from the West
riding in a horse-drawn carriage
along cobbled streets
imagining my elegant grandmother
cigarette holder in her long fingers
three husbands to her name
a will stronger than any man's
being 'firm but fair' with the servants
hard as nails
but spoiling my mother
her only child

waiting at tables
during the occupation
hiding from the Gestapo
as she'd once hidden
from the Bolsheviks
she waves a picture of the Virgin Mary
under a German officer's nose
till he lets her and my mother pass
she's used to getting her own way
somehow it works

years later
the two of us pitched
in a furious battle of wills
and rivalry
over my mother
Babcia told me she would haunt me
when she died
that I'd be sorry then
but I never was

though now
I wish I'd been less afraid
and known her better
I remember the shabbiness
of her London home:
she is still giving my mother
endless gifts
slipping packets of honey cakes
into her net bag
but now it's her blue persian cat
she spoils the most
smiling into its smouldering orange eyes

48

ZOMO riot police

STRIKE

It's getting hotter
I'm in Gdańsk
among the red brick spires
I've seen nothing
of the strike at the shipyard
road blocks everywhere
ZOMO's in grey uniforms
patrol in twos and threes
everyone keeps telling me who they are
I get impatient and say I know
try to explain about the British equivalent
the men who ride in unmarked vans
do they believe me?
somehow they've heard of British bobbies
being gentlemen
helping old ladies cross the street
anything else they've read in papers
and here no one believes
in what they read
even if it's sometimes the truth

WSZYSCY JESTEŚMY ODPOWIEDZIALNI ZA POLSKĘ

50

Gdańsk: Lenin shipyard, birthplace of Solidarność

after the strike is broken up

it's as if nothing had happened
I walk past the shipyard
along with other tourists
or passers-by

it's as if I'm walking across
an empty stage
staring at the backdrop
of poplar trees and blocks of flats

the gates of the Lenin Shipyard
fresh flowers laid at the foot
of the three giant crosses
erected by the workers right outside it
like discarded props
or painted scenery

what did I expect?
to hear the sound of running footsteps
crowds scattered by police
stirring speeches and cheers
still echoing

I stand there amazed
sneak photos of the shipyard gate
a military secret
screened all over the world
then further on, take pictures
of cranes against the skyline
another of those
forbidden things
people do just the same

Babcia z tulipanami - tulip woman

all day in the sun
the old woman sits
under the walkway
beside her bucket of tulips
the brightest things in the street
selling them in small bunches
three or five at a time
how can you feed anyone
on a bucket a day
of red tulips

Lake at Żuromino

in her parents' house
in the still flat countryside
by the big lake
we're alone at last
I turn to her
but she turns away

nothing I say makes any difference
at night
she keeps an axe under our bed
she starts to shake
each time the wind sighs
or the martins chatter
in the mud nests
they've built in the eaves
in the end I hold and stroke her
till she falls asleep

in the morning
she sleeps late
reads old newspapers
smokes cigarettes
avoids my eyes

some afternoons
she teaches me to play cards
I teach her to write English limericks
we go out to buy fresh farm milk
and eggs from the village
the milk's all right
we put it out on the sill
to make real yoghurt
but the eggs taste awful
like rotten fish
we joke about this
then suddenly I find I can't stop crying

Old and new co-existing

I often think of the young skier
her still-warm body
buried so quickly
did she call out as she fell
her cries
lost in the immense silence
muffled by softly falling snow
they must have found her by now

WSZYSCY JESTEŚMY ODPOWIEDZIALNI ZA POLSKĘ

Mosque at Kruszyniany

be careful what you say to others
especially to those you care about
words have wings
they settle in the branches
of your life
they sing loudly
till their song becomes your own

the lies you tell
have a way of preying
on your mind
they swoop down unexpectedly
from nowhere
they carry off
pieces of your heart
between their claws

Dreaming of freedom

before I left
my mother said
don't tell anyone
about, you know...
your life

it would get round
the whole of Warsaw
we'd never live it down
although we haven't lived there
for over 30 years

is that all you care about
your reputation, I argued back
but it's you I'm trying to protect
she said, *you don't know*
what people there are like

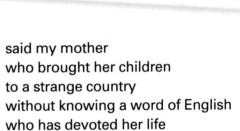

said my mother
who brought her children
to a strange country
without knowing a word of English
who has devoted her life
to keeping us safe from harm

stay in the golden cage, my dove
stay in the golden cage
it's made for you with all my love
my little dove

62

Folk musicians

among all the words here
like a dear face
lost in a crowd
where are you
'my lover'?
I can only find
'my friend'
to say
you belong in another place
in my step-motherland
with other words and codes,
other badges, or graffiti
on other demonstrations
you don't exist
here at all
except in a whisper

WSZYSCY JESTEŚMY ODPOWIEDZIALNI ZA POLSKĘ

what's in a name?
people can reach their own conclusions
why spell it out
when people might despise you?
let's stay in the golden cage, my love
I hear an old voice inside my head
is it worth mentioning now
when each day she slips further away
from me
yet the more I say *my friend*
the truer it becomes

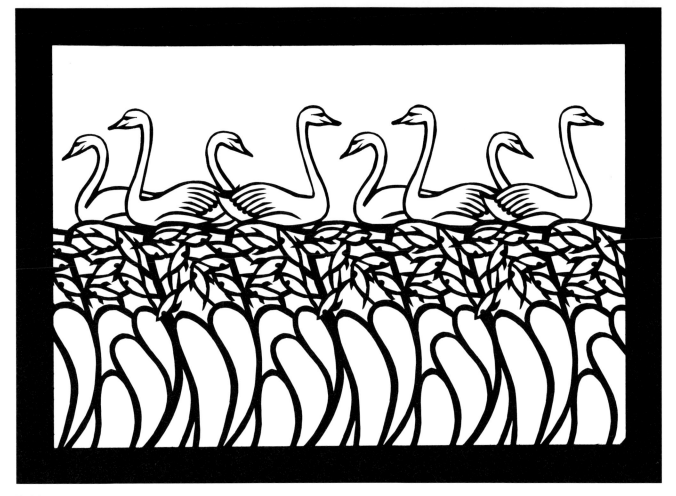

Baltic swans

BALTIC SWANS

for Zosia

Out of the summer sky
Huge snowflakes   settling on the sea
Floating palaces of one-time elegance
That bob up and down   on gentle waves
White as marble against green lawns
White on petrol blue
The swans glide towards the shore
As if nothing could harm them,
Extend their graceful necks
To wolf down the holidaymakers' handouts
Bread and ice-cream cones
Without standing on ceremony at all.

Don't they know   the sea is sick?
Contagious under its smooth surfaces
It has already spewed up
Thousands of dead eels and fish.

66

It no longer belongs
To the people with ice-creams
Who still come to watch   from the safety of the pier.
Some of the reckless ones
Lie in the sand next to it   go bathing.
They can't believe
The coastline has been taken
Away from them again
Only this time the occupying force   has poured in under cover
Not soldiers
But tons of waste
Entering fathoms deep.
On a summer's day   who wants to shout at their kids
'Stay out of the water!'
Or remember the truckloads of dead fish
When the beach had to be cleared.

The people come to see
If the swans are still there
And the swans swim   right up to the people
Gliding on the water
As if nothing could harm them.

Gypsies working the tourists

another friend, H
arrives from Sheffield
doesn't speak a word of Polish
what am I going to do with her?!

but she's got a musical ear
learns fast
listening with an open heart –
somebody from England
who *wants* to know!

impossible to imagine a scene like this
in Sheffield or London
neither of us could ever afford it
we sit in the most expensive hotels
like characters in a play

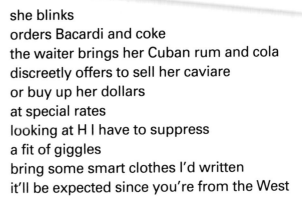

she blinks
orders Bacardi and coke
the waiter brings her Cuban rum and cola
discreetly offers to sell her caviare
or buy up her dollars
at special rates
looking at H I have to suppress
a fit of giggles
bring some smart clothes I'd written
it'll be expected since you're from the West

WSZYSCY JESTEŚMY ODPOWIEDZIALNI ZA POLSKĘ

70

Kayak excursion

MAZURY

thank heavens we're out of the city
it's summer
and my mountain guide auntie
has turned captain
as we canoe across the lakes

she and her elegant friend
in the straw hat
the two older ladies
with whom we try to keep up

on a tiny island
H and I build a camp fire
I haven't done this
since I was a child
we manage to light it
with a single match

my auntie teaches us a song
H thinks she's learning
a traditional Polish folksong

WSZYSCY JESTEŚMY ODPOWIEDZIALNI ZA POLSKĘ

actually it's in Russian
tells the story of the ze-ka
prisoners rounded up
during one of the purges
herded on board a ship
bound for Magadan

in the morning
we bathe
in the green stillness
of the lake
no sound
except the splash
of a grebe
diving under water
among the lilies
we think it's vanished
it stays under so long
only to pop up again
in an altogether different place

72

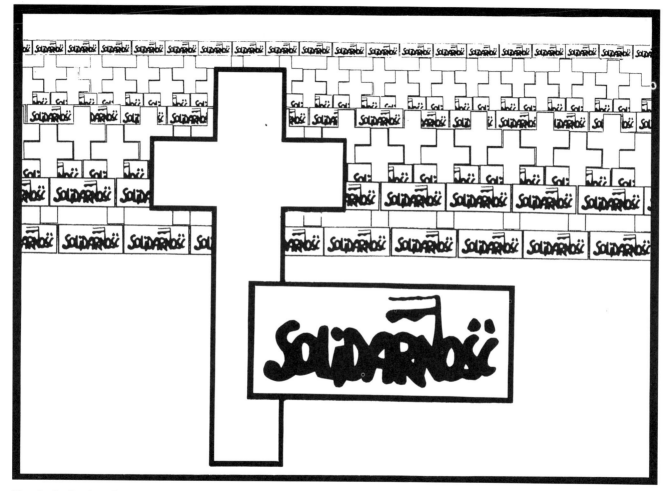

The Catholic church supported the struggle for freedom

reluctantly,
I take H to St. Stanisław's Church
where Father Popiełuszko lies buried
I've become like the locals
who complain
about coachloads of pilgrims
creating traffic jams round it
every weekend
besides I've seen it all before
didn't I grow up on a diet of martyrs
and dead heroes?

facing inwards
on the iron railings
of the church grounds
hang the banners
prohibited anywhere else
I translate the slogans for H

WSZYSCY JESTEŚMY ODPOWIEDZIALNI ZA POLSKĘ

everything from let's fight alcoholism
to workers' rights,
demands for pluralism
and pledges of devotion
to Our Lady, Queen of Poland

We walk past the stone tablets
each one bears the name of a camp
like Treblinka or Oświęcim
states the number of people killed
which the Germans recorded
meticulously
and then the stone for Katyń
next to them
it looks like another Nazi camp
but there is no number on it
suddenly tears are streaming
down my cheeks

From wooden huts to concrete blocks

KRYSTYNA

Streetlight glows on the metal crucifix
where her God hangs
too busy saving the world
to hear her voice
like the planners
who've left her hanging
suspended in this concrete box
half way into the sky
on the eleventh floor.

She knows if she were to shout
or scream from her window
the din of the traffic below
would carry away her choice words

till they fell
bursting open
against more concrete.
Instead she hums behind closed doors
and windows
a low drone
more like a growl
sounds you wouldn't call a song.
But it's her song
her grey lullaby
as evening falls.

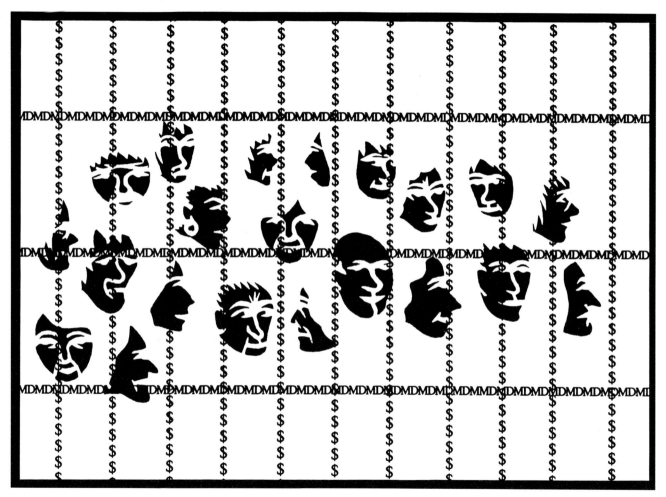

Dreaming of western prosperity

THEY WANT TO BE NORMAL

everyone keeps telling me
they want to be normal
I grew up afraid
I'd never be normal
knowing difference
till it became a second skin
but this is not what they mean

*just once before I die
a doctor says to me
I'd like to live a normal life
I don't need furs or perfumes
she tells me
they can keep them
I just want to go in a shop
to buy ham when I want it
plan a meal
for three months before I die
that's what I'd like*

then the taxi driver is telling me
*you wouldn't get this in a normal country
they've been repairing that bridge
since when
this fucked-up socialist system
when something finally happens
everyone's so pleased
they start handing out medals
congratulating one another
as though they'd been in bloody labour*

WSZYSCY JESTEŚMY ODPOWIEDZIALNI ZA POLSKĘ

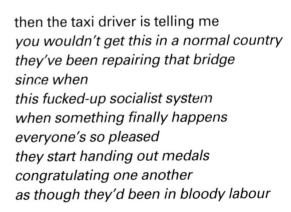

WORDS DANCE ON MY SKIN

words dance on my skin
roll down my back
like drops of warm rain
drench me from head to toe

words rush over my head
like swallows at evening

in trams and on buses
words press against me
push and squeeze past me
like tired people in a hurry

in the street
words saunter past me
young and cocky like soldiers
sweating inside their uniforms

79

words whisper in the branches
of pine trees
jump over gravestones
like squirrels
playing hide and seek
with my memory

out in the open
words shake the tops
of poplars
scatter over the flat brown earth
brush my face twice
like a kiss on either cheek

deciding which words to take home
is an impossible task
but they don't all fit
in my rucksack

I wrap some words carefully
in between jumpers and towels
I don't even notice
I'm taking others
they'll pour out
of my socks and shoes
like grains of dust or sand
when I get home

at the airport
under the sign
which says no firearms
or pure spirit
I walk through
trying not to draw attention
to myself
carrying out over my limit
of Polish words

Field with stooks

finally I'm flying back
among the businessmen and tourists
those leaving loved ones
those about to be reunited
those already gearing themselves up
for months of work
in cafés, chip-bars
cleaning houses

above the green squares
on Europe's chess board
eating salmon in plastic containers
drinking free champagne
I'm flying back again
to where simply by being different
you run the risk
of having burning rags posted
through your letter box

where old people, too scared
of running up their bills
to turn on an electric fire,
die from the cold each year
despite mild winters
without 'real snow'
where the divide
between have
and have-not
grows deeper with each minute
like a volcanic rift
running right through the land
where on the brimming shelves in shops
I'll find everything
including Polish sausages and ham
or shoes marked 'Made in Poland'
back again in my normal life

we are all responsible for Poland

WSZYSCY JESTEŚMY ODPOWIEDZIALNI ZA POLSKĘ

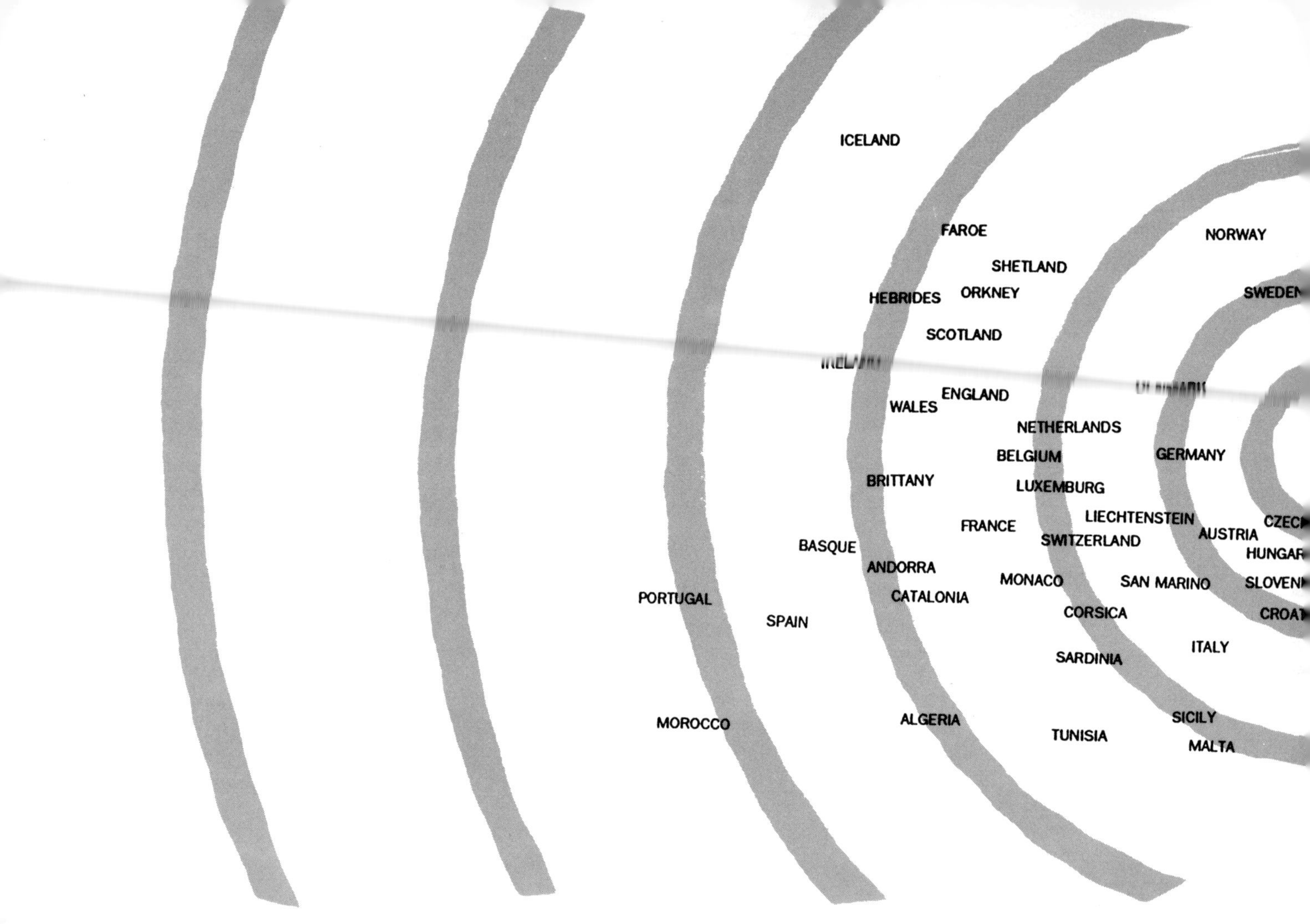

ICELAND

FAROE

SHETLAND

HEBRIDES   ORKNEY

SCOTLAND

IRELAND

ENGLAND

WALES

BRITTANY

BASQUE

ANDORRA

PORTUGAL   CATALONIA

SPAIN

MOROCCO

NETHERLANDS

BELGIUM

LUXEMBURG

FRANCE

SWITZERLAND

MONACO

CORSICA

SARDINIA

ALGERIA

TUNISIA

NORWAY

SWEDEN

GT BRITAIN

GERMANY

LIECHTENSTEIN

AUSTRIA   CZECH

HUNGAR

SAN MARINO   SLOVEN

CROAT

ITALY

SICILY

MALTA

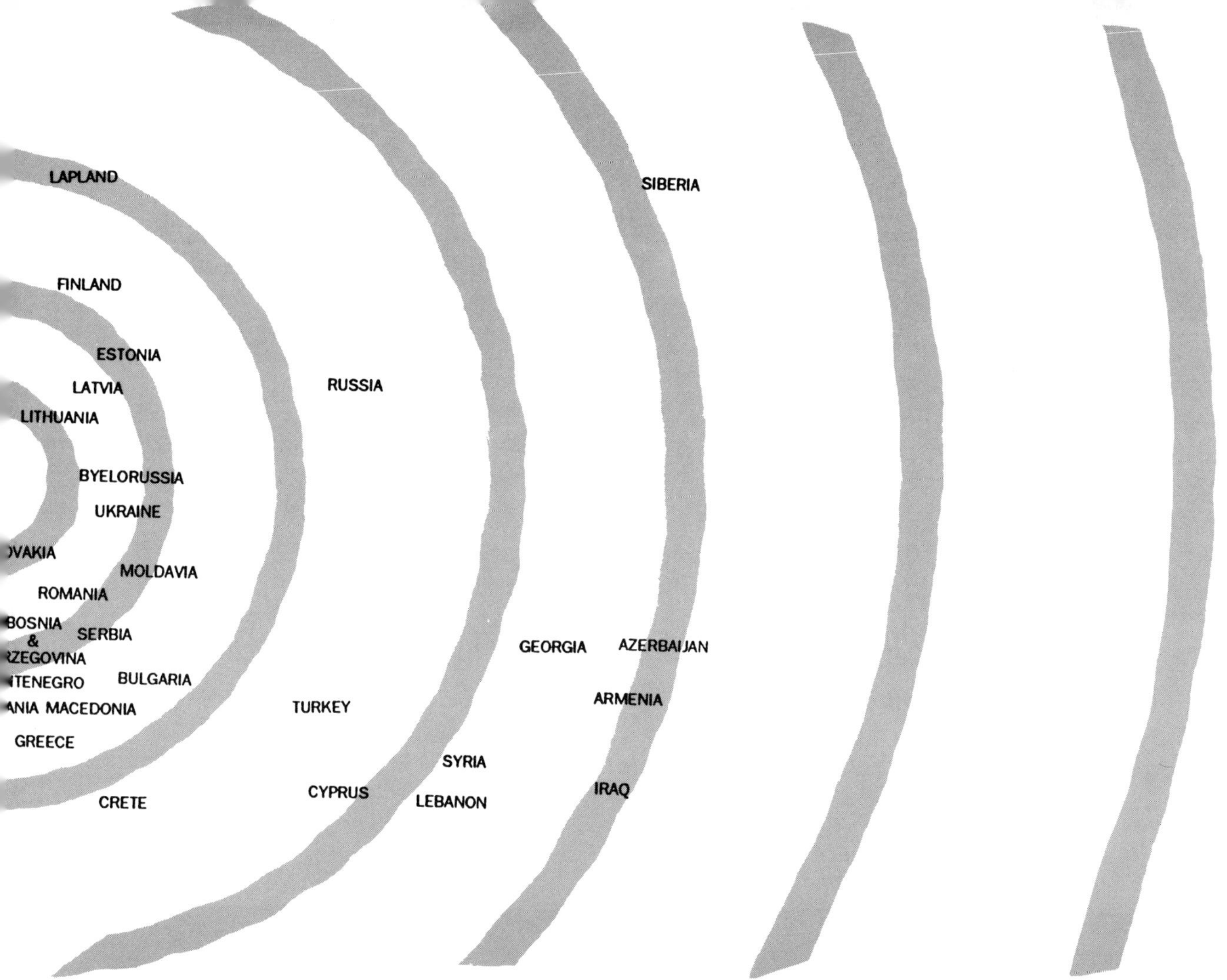

LAPLAND

SIBERIA

FINLAND

ESTONIA

LATVIA

RUSSIA

LITHUANIA

BYELORUSSIA

UKRAINE

OVAKIA

MOLDAVIA

ROMANIA

BOSNIA
&
RZEGOVINA

SERBIA

GEORGIA   AZERBAIJAN

TENEGRO

BULGARIA

ARMENIA

ANIA MACEDONIA

TURKEY

GREECE

SYRIA

CYPRUS   LEBANON

IRAQ

CRETE

after

I noticed the change in people's faces

THE EMPEROR REGRETS

a spokesperson from the Imperial palace
has confirmed
the Emperor now admits
he was not wearing new clothes
after all

this has come as no surprise
whatsoever to the majority
of his citizens
who shrug and say:
what difference does it make
after all these years
given the price of a kilo
of just about anything nowadays
which we still can't afford

a few foreign journalists
have been caught off guard
several male artists have gone back
to painting large canvasses

of female nudes
now the subject of 'Nudity'
is no longer officially proscribed
many women have pointed out
that there is nothing original
or especially progressive about this

but news of the Emperor's decree
has come as a shock to some
including the middle-aged mother
of the child
who first cried out
'look, he's got nothing on!'
many years ago
since then
she has never seen
any of her children

recently, for the very first time
she was allowed
to visit their unmarked graves
in the countryside

Powązki: Catholic cemetery - grave of Grzegorz Przemek, picked up by police when celebrating after his end-of-school exams and beaten to death while in custody (1983)

they're changing the colour
of police uniforms in Poland
from 'socialist' grey to pre-war blue
even though its going to cost money
it's a dream of independence
coming true

but how do you change
the dreams of boys
who long for guns and fast car chases
power and the chance
to hide unmanly tears
behind a visor
or a riot shield

can you rinse out
the colour of blood
from any uniform
grey or blue

WSZYSCY JESTEŚMY ODPOWIEDZIALNI ZA POLSKĘ

92

First elections - vote for Gutman

DEUTSCHLAND, DEUTSCHLAND

how could I not be moved
seeing the thousands
of East German Trabants
queuing ready to cross the border
into the West
by scenes of reunited families
hugging each other crying for joy
after years of separation
grandparents and children
together for the first time

how could I not feel dread
hearing the anthem being sung
and sure enough within days
flashing across my T.V. screen
after the scenes of warm welcome
pictures of people in West Berlin
carrying banners which say
'Polen Raus! Türken Raus!'
'raus' I somehow know
even though I've never learnt German

WSZYSCY JESTEŚMY ODPOWIEDZIALNI ZA POLSKĘ

94

From a command to a market economy - the goods are here, but the prices sky-high

LIVE COVERAGE ON ENGLISH TV

the pleasant voice
of the male presenter
contrasts
with the voices of women
picked at random
for a few seconds
who somehow sound
less pleasant
than him
then the camera pans
down the backs of their legs
stops to stare
at their varicose veins

would you film your own mother
like this
somebody important
a head of state
or just old women
queuing in some remote place
like Poland

Kraków: historic city besieged by pollution

day after day
as if overnight
everyone's talking about us
hey, we're on the map!
even the rivers clogged up
and poisoned,
the faces of Kraków's statues
smudged by the smog
dogs dying from the air they breathe
babies and children
the ill and the old
without a chance
get a mention
mostly it's the victims
who are being *discovered* by the West
but hey, even briefly,
we're on the map!

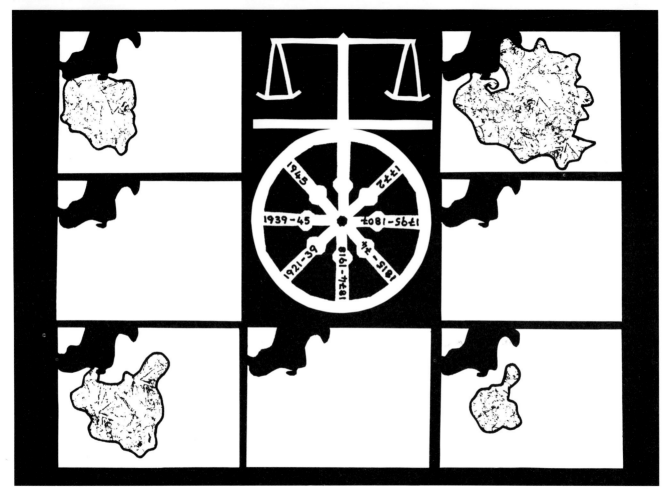

On and off the map

don't underestimate
what all this means to me
I'm sensitive about maps
I come from a country
which disappeared from the world map
for over a hundred years
whose borders have been shifted
backwards and forwards
rearranged by strangers many times

what's in a name
when is a nation a country
when is a country
a state?

when it's got a queen
or a president
or natural borders
or its own army
soldiers and checkpoints on its borders
or a symbol of its sovereignty
like a gold crown
or its own songs and customs
and great writers and artists
or when all the other countries
recognise it
take its views into account
treat it with respect

WSZYSCY JESTEŚMY ODPOWIEDZIALNI ZA POLSKĘ

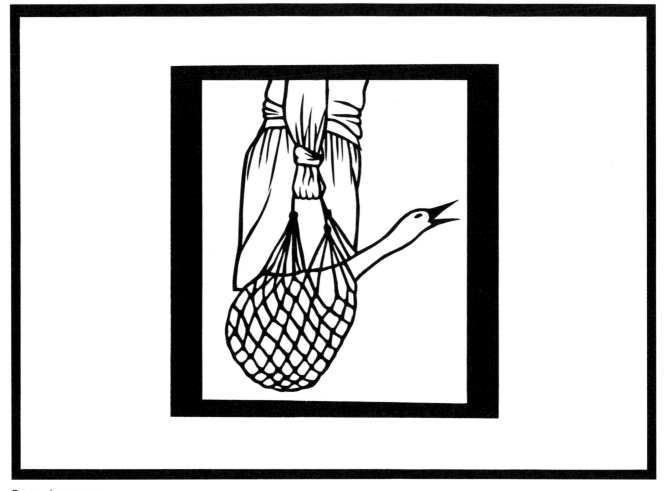

Protesting goose

Wałęsa came to London and kissed
Thatcherowa's hand
aren't Polish men gallant!

the English memsahib is rich and strong
like that other great English leader
Churchill, her hero,
who sat around
with the rest of the big boys
towards the end of World War Two
kicking around
spheres of influence
swapping countries
as they might have exchanged cigars
we'll have the Greeks ...
you'll have the Poles ...

don't kid yourself
Attlee was any better

they'd served their purpose
the Poles who'd fought
for 'your freedom and ours'
on the Allies' side
they weren't needed anymore

when Wałęsa arrived
Polish veterans joked
it's the electrician
come with a bill
for World War Two

today in the English papers
you'll read about the Poles
who can't even pay the interest
on their foreign debts
but who remembers the debt
owed to us by the West
how do you calculate interest
on so many lives

WSZYSCY JESTEŚMY ODPOWIEDZIALNI ZA POLSKĘ

Returning the pre-war names to Warsaw's streets

'THE DEATH OF SOCIALISM'

what will they do now
those chaps at the top
the Western generals and directors –
now they're slapping each other on the back
saying : good show, by jove
and gee whizz
we've won the Cold War –
if there aren't any Commie bastards
left to hate any more?

of course
you've got Blacks there
my aunt had said in Warsaw
from a thousand miles away
she'd grasped the situation
instantly

yes, in England
it's simple
there are always Blacks
and others
already singled out
so the chaps at the top
needn't worry
they'll soon find somebody
to protect their wives and children from
their property and their profits
so they can sleep easy
it'll be all right
it'll still be cricket

WSZYSCY JESTEŚMY ODPOWIEDZIALNI ZA POLSKĘ

104

Inflationary bus ticket, August 1989 – March 1990

NO COMPARISON

ever since I came back
from Poland
I get annoyed
when people make easy comparisons
between East and West
when for so long
there's been no comparison
to be made

like Polish banknotes,
for which people worked
doing two jobs at a time,
which did not convert
into anything
their value vanishing
the moment you left Poland
like fairy gold
turning to dust

WSZYSCY JESTEŚMY ODPOWIEDZIALNI ZA POLSKĘ

dreams forgotten
on waking
a life-time's experience
suddenly irrelevant
like qualifications
no one will recognise

I find these gaps far stranger
than the loss of a few hours
crossing time-zones
on jet planes
going much further
across the world

If only

IF ONLY
for anxious lovers everywhere

if only I'd taken things slower
or faster
been more or less romantic
bought her more roses, irises, daffodils
and chrysanthemums
loved her morning
noon and night
never held back

if only I'd needed her less
held my horses
or stuck to my guns

if only I'd been able to read her mind
known how to get past her defences
or seen right through her
if only I'd been more
or less understanding
if only I'd spoken up more
or listened harder

if only I'd stood on my head
and wiggled my ears
maybe we'd have lasted longer
or finished sooner
and maybe she'd still love me

SUDDENLY I AM VERY ILL

Suddenly I am very ill
more ill
than I have ever been before

a ghost with clammy hands
plays discordant notes
along my lower vertebrae

goblins fill my shoes and socks
with lead
making each step too heavy

I am living in slow-motion
moon-walking
while everyone else rushes past me

to get to work, meet their friends
reach a destination
at the appointed time

suddenly everything has stopped
inside my body
as if it were winter all year round

I can't get warm
only my head stays hot
as if a forest were burning inside it

what language do you dream in
people have often asked me
now I wonder

am I ill in Polish or English
but this is not a question
you can ask doctors

do you think it's something you caught
when you were over there
asks a nice woman at work

before I leave my job
I reassure her
that I'm not contagious

everyone's talking détente
while I have slipped
behind my own iron curtain
and can't escape

suddenly I am very ill
for a very long time
and now it's my turn
to receive postcards
instead of sending them

Bananas only for children with leukemia/banana skins all over Warsaw

BANANAS

everything's changing so fast
you wouldn't believe it
bananas all over Warsaw
clumps of yellow everywhere
like a strange bloom
out of season
the shops full of food
no queues any more
but no one can keep up
with the new prices
so in a way
things haven't changed that much

Crosses from Greek Catholic churches in the south

on the steps
of St. John's cathedral
or in the doorway opposite
young people with Aids sit
begging for money
from tourists and passers by

where are the medicines
they need?
where are their mothers or fathers,
the strong family ties
everyone takes for granted
close friends and neighbours?

where are the loving arms
in which every ill person
needs to be held?

Everyone's selling or buying something

you'd never recognise Warsaw
it's turned into a giant souk
in the subway
even children sell things
in the street it's the same
everyone's selling or buying something
there's fridges and radiators
straight from the factory
a boy with a guitar
and a pair of snow-white boots
wares laid out on camp beds
or blankets
or in the back of delivery vans

every morning
the covered wagons arrive
line up in rows
huge lumps of raw, red meat
chopped up with an axe
for the crowd of customers
pushing on all sides

WSZYSCY JESTEŚMY ODPOWIEDZIALNI ZA POLSKĘ

Zamość:rennaissance town of the south-east and birthplace of Rosa Luxemburg

FOR EWA WHO MISSES POLAND

You sit glued to the set
For hours
Watching English TV
Filling the room
With flickering blue light
And noise, the screech of brakes,
Buzzers, guns.
Flashing lights
New words and idioms
Served with pre-recorded laughs,
The glitter of rags-to-riches dreams
Fast-feed your hungry eyes
So that your eyes won't fill
With tears
Buckets and barrels of them
Your Polish tears
Salt as cucumber.

WSZYSCY JESTEŚMY ODPOWIEDZIALNI ZA POLSKĘ

118

EXCLUSIVE INTERVIEW WITH A WHITE EAGLE

– No, to tell you the truth
I wasn't pleased
When the first thing they decided
Was to stick this crown
Back on my head
I've always led an active life
Never been one
For sitting about
Looking regal
You try soaring to great heights
With this weight of gold
On your head.

– I know they mean well
I've watched over them for centuries
They're my people.

Of course I love them,
Watch them today
As they argue excitedly
Amongst themselves
About which design to choose
What exact shape the crown
Ought to be.

– I had hoped
For something different
I've flown the length of this country
From its mountains to the sea
And we are unanimous
Us birds.
From the smallest sparrow
To the tallest stork

119

From the city crow to the meadow lark
Including the farmyard hens and geese
The woodland cuckoo and the night owl
We agree on our priority
We want our sky back
The air we breathe
Where we coast and glide
Dip and dive
We want fresh rain and snow
The scent of lilac or pine
We want the butterflies and mites back
We want the air
Crisp as the truth again.
Same goes for the water
We want the fish swimming in it
And the land back,
The animals to roam,

Enough grain and plants to grow
Enough to feed every one of us.

– Yes, I remain optimistic
Things are changing so very much every day
I've always had faith
in those strange wingless creatures
Who are my people
Even at the worst moments
Down there
They have always carried freedom
Inside their hearts
They have not forgotten
To listen to us
They have never stopped loving our songs.

– Thank you.

KRYSIA ISN'T A FEMINIST

Krysia isn't a feminist
but
she went on the women's demonstration

Krysia says it might be all right
for Western women
maybe they have more time on their hands
what does she need feminism for
she's been doing a man's job
all her working life

Education not punishment - protests against changes in the abortion laws take place by the statue of Kopernik

but when she heard
of proposals to change the law
three years in prison
for a doctor performing an abortion
she went on the demonstration
and found herself shouting
with the other women

Krysia's husband, Tomek
was furious
a fine example for the children
their mother screaming
with a bunch of stupid women
she'd let him down
surely she understood
the need for unity
people had to stand by the Church
he shouted at her

Krysia started to answer him back
told Tomek it was a matter
of everyday survival
as well as the principle of it
did he want the country
going back to the Middle Ages?

then she stopped and looked at him
she was thinking about the abortion
she'd had
he hadn't said much at all then
he'd left it to her
to get on with it on her own
do the necessary
(after all, it was one of those 'women's things')

Krysia isn't a feminist
but

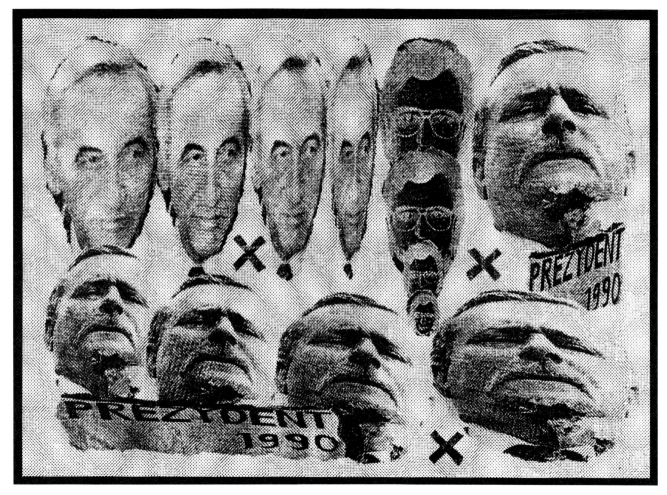

Presidential election - the differing fortunes of Mazowiecki, Tymiński and Wałęsa

FREEDOM

in the land
with an infinite array
of glossy matching coffee-table books
how to explain
authors being suddenly available
for the first time
Orwell, Pasternak, Miłosz
the nation's Nobel prize-winner,
historical works
along with pulp American
spy-thrillers
in which the KGB is always foiled
and pornography
books and books and books

yet there are those of us
who grew up in the West
never seeing
our own reflections
in all the increasingly high-tech
dazzling full-colour scenes
on video, film or TV ads
who hunger still
for images of our own lives
who have always had to
make mirrors
out of shadows and flickers
splinters and scraps
shards of glass

Powązki: communal cemetery - Warsaw uprising anniversary, monuments of Kiliński
battalion and Gozdawa sub-group - my mum's and dad's resistance units

[– – – –] [Ustawa z dnia 31.VII.1981r
o kontroli publikacji i widowisk,
art. 2 pkt. 3. (Dz. U. 20 poz. 99, zm:
1983 Dz. U. nr44, poz. 204)].

the simple pleasure of reading:
your mind's journey
of comprehension
unbroken
by the censor's odd punctuation
four dashes enclosed
in a square bracket
the date and legal abbreviations
a four-bar gate
at which the mind's traffic
got stopped
held up for years on end
left guessing
at missing paragraphs
or lines
this poem has not been monitored

WSZYSCY JESTEŚMY ODPOWIEDZIALNI ZA POLSKĘ

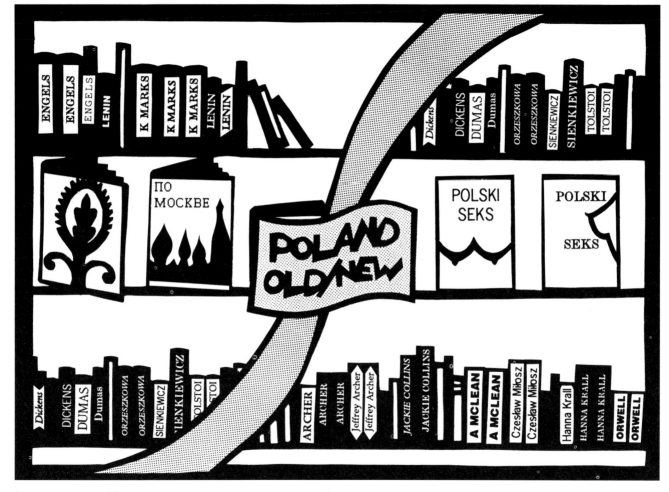

No more censorship

POLSKI SEKS

wouldn't it be good
if a title like this
meant what it said

wouldn't it be good
if there were magazines or books
about people reaching out to touch
one another
about how to cherish
every part of your lover's body
or how to cherish your own
inch by inch

magazines or books
that gave young people ideas
and old people reminders
that made their eyes light up –
with mischief and curiosity
sent their skin tingling
which turned everything upside down

and made everybody question
their habits and assumptions
made certain people
have to think again
made uncertain people
take giant leaps of faith
which included people
of all kinds

wouldn't that be good
instead of the usual pictures –
the ones we're hemmed in by
in the West –
of women and children,
occasionally men,
being used again and again
instead of humiliation
posing as nakedness
or brutality masquerading
as lust

WSZYSCY JESTEŚMY ODPOWIEDZIALNI ZA POLSKĘ

JUST BEING NORMAL

I grew up
running and skipping
in and out
of different worlds
humming to myself
the same way I ran
jumping over cracks
in the pavement

I could still remember then
the scaffolding on building sites
in post-war Warsaw
and maybe snow
so proud of my country
though each year
I remembered less and less of it

as I got older
I started longing
to eat fish fingers
and salted crisps
on white formica table-tops
instead of our old wooden one
to be the same
as everybody else
later for a man
to stand at my side
he had to be tall
with a real beard
that's all he had to do
stand there
flat as an icon
not his arms or his touch mattered then
just being normal

PRIDE AND SHAME

in the kitchen
where we washed
my father and his ex-colonel-
turned-plumber friend
fitted a new sink
the water ran mixing
hot and cold
out of the same tap
but it always seemed
like two separate streams
scalding my fingers

in the same way
pride and shame
splashed hot and cold
throughout my childhood
streaming through
both my daydreams
and my nightmares

later in life
I learned to carry difference
like a shield
a bright banner
a flaming torch
a shared look of understanding
I learned the strength
in numbers
the pride once more
of belonging
even if it meant
shutting others out

at the same time
shame taught me
to stand apart
to question everything
even if it has meant
life-long doubt

Powązki: Jewish cemetery

I can't bear
people who deny the extent
of anti-semitism
in Poland
before the war,
and during the war,
after the war
and today.

I also can't bear
people who know nothing at all
about Poland
and don't really care
dismissing all Poles
as a bunch of raving nationalists
and anti-semites.

They say, as you get older
you become less angry.
This does not seem
to be happening to me so far.

132

Joy is a fire that is stronger - proud to be Jewish, proud to be gay

DIFFERENCE

I have carried difference
like a dark secret
a flickering flame
a coded message
or a knife
learning and unlearning again
the lessons of pride and shame

these days
it is simply the backdrop
to everything I do
it is the sound
of my own footsteps
the light
behind my eyes
which I hide
only at my peril

WSZYSCY JESTEŚMY ODPOWIEDZIALNI ZA POLSKĘ

Jews Gypsies Slavs trade-unionists socialists communists homosexuals so-called criminals including lesbians
and prostitutes the physically disabled mentally handicapped the mad the old and the ill and the very young
female and male Jews Gypsies Slavs trade-unionists
socialists communists homosexuals so-called criminals
including lesbians and prostitutes the physically disabled
mentally handicapped   d the old and the ill and the
very young female   Jews Gypsies Slavs trade-
unionists social   munists homos uals so-called
criminals inclu   ians and prosti   e physically
disabled mentall   apped th   d and the
ill and the very you   ale   e   vpsies
Slavs trade-unionists   munists   exu-
als so-   ed criminals i   esbians and pr stitutes
the p.   disabl   ndicapped the mad
the old   i   e ver   female and male
Jews Gyps   rade-union.   ialists communists homose   so-called crimi   ding lesbians
and prostitutes the physically   mentally handicapped the mad the old ar   and the very young
female and male Jews Gyps.   Slavs trade-unionists
socialists communists homosexuals so-called criminals
including lesbians and prostitutes the physically disabled
mentally handicapped the mad the old and the ill and the
very young female and male Jews Gypsies Slavs trade-
unionists socialists communists homosexuals so-called

land-owners professionals army officers intellectuals
scientists civil servants white collar workers factory
workers artists writers religious people students
peasants farmers non-Russians Russians non-party
members and card carrying communists the old and the
ill and the very young female and male land-owners
professionals ar   ls scientists civil
servants whi   orkers artists
writers re   ple students peas ts farmers
non-Russi   ians non-party members and card
carrying   sts   d the ill and the very
young fe   nale   rofessionals army
officers i   ls scient   ts white collar
workers   vorker   riters religious
people stu   e   farm rs non-Russians
Russians non-   rs and card carrying communists the old and   young female and
male land-owner   rmy officers intellectuals scientis   vil servan   ite collar workers
factory work   artists w   religious people
students pe   farmers non   ians Russians non-
party membe   and card carry   mmunists the old
and the ill and the very young   le and male land-
owners professionals army officers intellectuals scientists civil servants white collar workers factory
workers artists writers religious people students
peasants farmers non-Russians Russians non-party

The disappeared

A SHORT LETTER TO LECH WAŁĘSA

In the Pink Paper, I read
you'd said homosexuals
and drug addicts
would be eliminated
from Polish society.

I thought to myself
a man like him
must know
how many millions of people
the Nazis eliminated –
they kept such precise records.
He must have relatives,
close friends or neighbours with relatives
who lost somebody;
like my two friends whose mothers'
entire families were wiped out.

A man with his experience
ought to know

WSZYSCY JESTEŚMY ODPOWIEDZIALNI ZA POLSKĘ

how many millions of people
the Soviets eliminated –
though their records are not so precise.
He's bound to have –
I thought to myself –
relatives, close friends or neighbours
with relatives they never saw again.

In the Pink Paper today, I read
a disclaimer
nobody could actually say
who'd heard you say those things.
So I am glad,
I hope you never even think them.

Dear Lech
Is there a single Pole in the world
who does not remember somebody?
How could anyone in Poland
ever use the word eliminate again?

Świder, near Warsaw, where my mum lived

in months of drought
a single match
can set alight
a whole forest
burning everything
in its path

in adverse circumstances
there is a disease
which spreads like wildfire
robbing people of joy

initial symptoms include
dryness of mouth
profuse sweating
of the palms or underarms
terrible trembling
and an empty space
near the abdomen

WSZYSCY JESTEŚMY ODPOWIEDZIALNI ZA POLSKĘ

transmitted
by the most casual
of encounters
picked up
from a single word
or look
its name is fear

today I read
there are already
five lesbian and gay magazines
in Poland
I remembered
that there's an antidote to fear
it can be found in everyday life
made from natural reactions
like shaking with anger
lifting your head in pride
and holding hands with hope
it is called love.

Graffiti: Poland for ~~Poles~~ people

they harm themselves
the most
those Poles arriving
in the West
who turn their noses up
at the immigrants
already settled there
hoping, in vain,
to win favour
with their hosts
who will despise them anyhow

who better than Europe's Blacks
or Irish, Turks ...
to understand
the Polish woman or man

from a country
of nearly all white people
where they could never
make ends meet
where their children
were beaten in police custody
the Poles made to feel
ashamed of their country's poverty?

who better to understand this
than Europe's Blacks?

WSZYSCY JESTEŚMY ODPOWIEDZIALNI ZA POLSKĘ

Sandomierz: historic town of the south-east

RIDDLE

The monster wears a business suit
He acts benign, yet he's astute
Helping democracy take root –
He's from the West
So he knows the best –
Holding out cash with his right hand.
His smile is bland.
He says:
"I'm going to give you foreign aid
To help clear up
The mess you've made
Of your environment."

The monster boasts that he is green
But watch him closely, have you seen
He's offering cash to that same land
But with his other hand.
His smile stays bland.

"Poor little country, you'll be paid
To take our toxic waste away
Our:
Partly processed sewage,
Radioactive garbage,
Electronic bits and pieces,
Liquid chemicals and faeces.
It's known to us as a fair trade
To help clear up
The mess we've made
In our environment."

Now that you know the monster's game,
It shouldn't take long
To guess his name.

Queue for shares

naturalists have discovered
a breed of leopard
able to change its spots rapidly
at large in major Polish cities
and continuing to make its home
in the most comfortable apartments or villas
Panthera Pardus Nomenklaturus
the high-ranking official
who has no difficulty talking
to businessmen and counterparts abroad
in the universal language
of money
which he has managed to accumulate
over the years

converting now
with astonishing ease
from hard-line Marxist Leninism
to cut-throat market economics

but further investigation
suggests the naturalists have got it wrong
this is no leopard
but a hyena
wearing the same stripes
all along

WSZYSCY JESTEŚMY ODPOWIEDZIALNI ZA POLSKĘ

KATYŃ

A letter arrives from Poland
the stamp has a cross on it
over the cross
the year: 1940
with one word: Katyń.
It has taken fifty years
to produce this stamp.

To the reader
who doesn't know
what Katyń means:
imagine the tip of an iceberg
strata of ice
hidden from your view,
each layer representing a decade.
Think of the lives lost
every decade
in executions, prisons and camps.

Or: You are a long way from home.
You are walking
through beautiful woods
but your hands have been tied
behind your back.
Snow still lies on the ground,
a spring sun shines
through the branches of conifers.
If you try to shout or call out
someone will tie an overcoat
around your head
or cram sawdust into your mouth.
If you slacken your pace
they will prod you
with a bayonet.
Imagine silence
after a gun has been fired
into the back of your head.

Imagine cynicism
dug as deep as the pit
into which hundreds of bodies are thrown.
Think how many lies
had to be shovelled in
to cover up these bodies.
How many more lies
and how much more cynicism it took
to cover those first lies,
like the rows of spruce saplings
planted to hide the graves
so this area would blend in
with the rest of the forest.
The number of people
needed to spread the lies
important people
in the highest places
as well as ordinary folk
who lived nearby.
The terror which forced
truthful people to lie.

Russians told the lies.
Americans and Britons
agreed to believe them
even though they knew better,
had the facts before them.
All of them tried to silence
those tiresome troublemakers the Poles
who kept on asking the same questions
about Katyń
who kept its memory alive
often by word of mouth
for fifty years.

Katyń is the name of a forest
near Smoleńsk, in the Soviet Union
where four thousand Polish officers
were murdered.
It is only one of the places
where mass murder was committed.
In a country renowned for its postage stamps
it has taken half a century
to commemorate Katyń.

Queuing for visas at the British embassy takes several days -
one person in fifteen is finally accepted as a "bona-fide visitor"

THE HUNGRY OF EASTERN EUROPE

in recent years
there weren't many immigrants
in Poland –
who in their right mind
would emigrate from the West
and no one from the East
was allowed to

now the hungry
of Eastern Europe
wander into each others' countries
wind up in Poland
the last stop
they can make –
nobody in the West
wants them

Bociek - stork

a letter arrives from Georgia!
posted in the old way
by someone travelling to the West
it bears an English stamp

outside my window
lies the world of fax machines
satellite communications
but I want to jump up and down
because a letter has reached me
from Georgia!

I have written three times
but received no reply
writes my niece
with the jet-black hair
by a quirk of family history
we're almost the same age
she sends me a photo
of the one time we met
many years ago in Poland

there I am with long hair
wearing a flowery dress
I remember us
sneaking off together
for a smoke
when her grandmother
wasn't looking

after years of not daring
to write directly
for fear of the trouble
a foreign letter could bring them
what on earth do I answer?

I come from a people
scattered across the world
forced many times
into exile or emigration
deported and resettled
divided and kept apart

I'm only now piecing together
a picture of my whole family
all the forbidden relations
non-conformers and family skeletons
lurking in cupboards
as well as the highly respectable,
those who took to drink
went mad, the suicides,
artists, revolutionaries, lovers
who acted with courage
or ingenuity
the Jewish and the Russian
and Georgian connections
severed for so long

I write:
I have changed a lot
my hair is short
I no longer smoke
I have been very ill
I would like to know
more about your country

so far I have only imagined
sunlight bouncing
off the Caucasian mountains
falling into blue lakes or sea,
there are the shells
smooth as porcelain
my dad's mum –
Babcia with the gentle grey eyes
and soft, sing-song accent –
brought back for us
all the way from the Black Sea,

on television I saw the pictures
of people mourning
those shot by the troops in Tbilisi –
I know of times
when if a woman's husband
was arrested
she would divorce him straight away –
her only chance to protect
her children from association
with an Enemy of the State

ever since I can remember
you had to be careful
what you said
to whom
to Germans, to Russians,
worst of all to other Poles
to immigration in strange lands,
Kennkarte,
forged papers, false identities,
somehow blurred
with maintaining appearances
keeping up with the Sąsiędzkis
where I come from
so many stories
remain untold

I am still piecing together
a picture of my whole self
the parts just as real
as the loving daughter
with a university degree

I want to ask:
do you think it's possible
could we live to see a time
when there'll be no need
for any more lies
when all the stories
can be told?

GLOSSARY AND BACKGROUND INFORMATION

ATTLEE, Clement: British Prime Minister (Labour) met with H. Truman and J. Stalin in July/Aug of 1945 in Potsdam, after the end of WW2 to agree on Germany's future and Poland's borders.

BABCIA: granny, old woman.

BANKOWY, Plac: Bank Square, in Warsaw.

BŁYSKAWICA (lightening): home-made automatic pistol used in the **Warsaw Uprising** and featured on pages 11 and 33. In the **Ghetto Uprising** there may have been no more than one of these.

CHURCHILL, Winston. British Prime Minister (Conservative). Following secret talks in Teheran in 1943, Churchill, Roosevelt and Stalin met in Yalta in Feb. 1945 where they discussed Poland's borders. Their decisions were confirmed at the Potsdam conference.

CIUPAGI: highlanders' axes

DZIERŻYŃSKI, Feliks: Polish Communist who headed Internal Security (Cheka) under Stalin and was responsible for the deaths and detention of countless people. A hated figure, whose statue in Warsaw was considered an affront. Various tricks were played on this monument, such as painting the hands red or leaving faeces at the foot of it.

ELECTIONS, FIRST: Early summer 1989 saw Poland's first post-war elections in which not all candidates were approved by the party. As 60% of parliamentary seats were still reserved for the party it was not a completely free election, but a step on the way to one (expected in spring 1991).

ELECTIONS, PRESIDENTIAL: In autumn 1990 Poles the world over voted for a new president. The three main contenders were **Lech Wałęsa** of **Solidarność**; Tadeusz Mazowiecki, first non-communist prime minister of post-war eastern Europe; Stanisław Tymiński, a business-man living abroad who promised unrealistic prosperity. Such were the hardships resulting from the government's economic reforms that people responded to Tymiński's promises and voted him in ahead of Mazowiecki. In the second ballot **Wałęsa** won decisively. He has continued Mazowiecki's economic policies.

HUNGRY OF EASTERN EUROPE: others try to reach the West by going South, via Hungary.

KATYŃ: One of the sites where thousands of Polish POW's were murdered by the Soviets in 1940 as part of a systematic campaign to eliminate all potential leaders such as officers, intellectuals, etc. This was in keeping with the Soviet - Nazi pact of 1939 which aimed at a carve up of Poland by the two powers after the war. When Hitler reneged on this pact in 1941 by invading the Soviet Union, Stalin switched sides and joined the Allies. The mass graves of Katyń were discovered in the USSR by retreating German soldiers in 1943. The Soviets blamed the murders on the Nazis. When the Poles refuted this, the Soviets accused the Poles of collaboration with the Germans. Katyń became a pretext for the Soviet Union to sever relations with the exiled Polish government in London, paving the way for a new Communist government to be imposed in Poland after the war.

KOPERNIK, Mikołaj (Nicolaus Copernicus): 1473 - 1543 astronomer who put forward the revolutionary (at that time) theory that the earth orbits the sun. He is seen in Poland as a symbol of enlightenment and reason.

KURONIOWKA: free soup named after Jacek Kuroń, formerly a notable dissident, latterly government minister responsible for social welfare.

LUXEMBURG, Rosa: Polish-Jewish revolutionary, active in Germany at the time of the Russian revolution.

MAP of POLAND: From 1795 to 1918 Poland was partitioned by the Prussian, Russian and Austro-Hungarian Empires. Polish autonomy, culture and language were to varying degrees brutally suppressed. From 1815 to 1874 the Russians created a token Polish state with no real power. Poland regained its independence from 1918 to 1939. Then throughout WW2 it was occupied by Germany and the Soviet Union. After the war the Allies agreed to the Soviet Union's continuing occupation of Polish territories and gave Poland a swathe of pre-war Germany.

MAZURY: Mazurian lake district in North East Poland.

PLAC ZAMKOWY: Castle Square in Warsaw's beautiful Old Town, reconstructed after the war.

POPIEŁUSZKO, Father Jerzy: Catholic Priest with oppositional views, murdered by police in 1984.

POWĄZKI: a district of Warsaw famous for its cemetaries. Biggest of these are the historic Roman Catholic and Jewish cemeteries. Dependent for their upkeep and conservation on donations and private initiatives, the current state of these two burial grounds reflects the fortunes of their respective communities. Clustered round these are several small Moslem and Evangelical grave-yards. A mile up the road is the big communal cemetery which houses the dead of two world wars and earlier uprisings. On August 1st, anniversary of the **Warsaw Uprising**, it is full of candles, flowers and people.

RELIGIONS. Throughout the Middle Ages and Renaissance, Poland's unusual liberalism encouraged thriving communities of Jews, Orthodox Christians, Lutherans, Moslems and others, attracting heretics and outcasts from other European countries. Towards the end of the C16th, religious tolerance gradually declined with the ascendency of the Jesuits, although Poland remained a religiously mixed country until WW2. The extermination of the Jews and other minorities, the reorganisation of boundaries and resettlement of people after the war has resulted in an almost homogenously Roman Catholic country.

SECTION 28 of the local Government Act 1988 in Britain: was designed to prevent local authorities from developing their equal opportunites policies to cover sexuality by forbidding them to "promote homosexuality", creating a climate of fear and uncertainty. However, the lesbian and gay community responded with even greater activity and solidarity to oppose this legislation.

SOLIDARNOŚĆ (SOLIDARITY): Starting in 1980 with a strike at the Gdańsk shipyard, Solidarność rapidly became a mass movement and a free trade union with a membership of millions. Its major strength was the bringing together of workers and intellectuals in the struggle against tyranny. Suppressed with the imposition of martial law in December 1981, it rose again to prominence in the late 1980's, when it fielded candidates for the permitted 40% of seats in the parliamentary elections of 1989, all of whom were successful. Associated with Solidarność from its earliest days and its most charismatic leader is Nobel prize-winner **Lech Wałęsa**, an electrician from the Gdańsk shipyard. His daring leadership, particularly in setting up round table talks in spring 1989 between Solidarność and the communist government, has been key in re-introducing democratic government to Poland, with knock-on effects in the whole of eastern Europe.

TRABANT: East German make of car.

UMSCHLAGPLATZ: The station depot at Stawki St. in Warsaw turned into an assembly point for mass deportations by the Nazis during the war.

UPRISING, GHETTO: started against the nazis on 19th April 1943, the day the Germans planned to finish the task of annihilating the Warsaw ghetto. Members of Żydowska Organizacja Bojowa (Jewish Fighting Organisation) numbered 220 - more volunteered, but there were no more guns. They held out until 10th May. While there was never a possibility of defeating the Germans at this stage, the insurgents succeeded in their aim of making a powerful stand for freedom, honour and humanity. None of them was taken alive.

UPRISING, WARSAW: started against the nazis on 1st August 1944, at a time when Germany was already losing the war. Many thousands of fighters of Armia Krajowa (Home Army) and affilliated organisations were involved. Despite the initial possibility of success and the heroism of both the resistance and the civilian population, by 3rd October lack of essential supplies or significant allied assistance in the face of the nazis' superior fire power had ground the city into defeat. The survivors were taken prisoner and most of the city was reduced to rubble (see poem on page 11, picture on page 25). Soviet forces, camped all the while across the river, just watched.

WAŁĘSA, Lech: see **Solidarność** and **Elections**.

WYCINANKA: papercut.

ŻUROMINO: one of the Kashubian lakes, North West Poland.

About the Artist

Jola Scicińska was born and brought up Polish in London, a fact that features strongly in her work which is based on the Polish peasant art of papercutting. This she uses either alone or in conjunction with collage, hand paper-making or photocopy-montage. Her researches have introduced her to Jewish, Chinese and Scandinavian papercutting and some influence of these is reflected in current work. The underlying theme of all her work is a celebration of people and their surroundiings as one of the necessary steps to end all oppression. Since she began showing her work in 1983, she has been involved in numerous shows in Britain and Poland, including five solo exhibitions. Scicińska has work in private collections in Australia, Germany, Italy, Poland, UK and USA. Her illustrations have appeared in a number of magazines and books. She is a member of Bigos – Artists of Polish Origin, which recently had a successful touring show in Poland. At the time of going to press, Bigos is touring an Arts Council funded made-to-measure show throughout Britain.

About the Author

Born in Warsaw, Poland in 1953, Maria Jastrzębska came to England as a small child. Her first collection of poetry 'Six and a half poems' came out in 1986. Since then she has been a member of the editiorial group which produced 'Forum Polek - The Polish Women's Forum' a bi-lingual anthology of women's work. Her poetry has appeared in the anthologies, The New British Poetry (Paladin 1988), Naming The Waves (Virago 1988) and Serious Pleasure (Sheba 1989). Her poems, articles, reviews and translations from the Polish have also appeared in magazines such as Spare Rib, Writing Women, Gen, Trouble and Strife, Spinster, Literary Review and Argo. She has taught for many years, working with both young people and adults, and is a trainer of Women's Self Defence. For two years she has struggled with M.E. and intends to recover.

About the book

Our artistic partnership goes back over many years. For this book we exchanged photographs, swapped anecdotes and snippets of family history, delighted in learning new Polish expressions, slang and songs and pooled our knowledge of Polish culture, politics and history. Right from the start we decided to challenge the conventional relationship between writer and illustrator, so that the pictures and poems, while at times complementary, each tell their own story, sharing equal importance and value.

The pictures in this book were made using the techniques of papercutting, collage, photocopy-montage and photography. Some of the patterned papers were printed specially, others were made by multiple photocopying of a dot screen. A few backgrounds were generated using a computer. Apart from the simple photographs, all pictures involve some cut or torn paper and none of them are drawings or paintings.

The poems can be read singly or chronologically as part of a narrative.

An installation based on some of the poems and pictures was shown at Community Copyart in Autumn 1990

OTHER BOOKS BY WORKING PRESS

Class Myths & Culture
Stefan Szczelkun

IF Comix numbers 1 & 2
Graham Harwood

Nothing Special
Micheline Mason

In Your Blood: Football Culture in the late 80's and early 90's
Richard Turner

Crossing Black Waters
ed. Allan de Souza & Shaheen Merali

The State of the Art & The Art of the State
Conrad Atkinson

The Unknown Deserter
Clifford Harper

The World Turned Upside Down
Clifford Harper

Frankie & Johnny
Clifford Harper

Household
Alison Marchant

FIST mega zine

ALSO AVAILABLE

Full-colour postcards of papercuts
set of 8 @ £2.00
send SAE with money to:
J. Sciciński, 24 Rancliffe Road, London E6 3HW

FORUM POLEK – POLISH WOMEN'S FORUM
bi-lingual anthology £5.95 (inc postage)
address as above

The Insider

Published in Warsaw, Poland

POLAND

THE REGION

COMMENTARY

CULTURE

BUSINESS

New English-language weekly newspaper

CONTENTS

after